On a Scary Scary Night

Can You See What I See?

On a Scary Scary Night

by Walter Wick

SCHOLASTIC INC.

New York   Toronto   London   Auckland   Mexico City   Sydney

New Delhi   Hong Kong   Buenos Aires

Published by Scholastic Inc.

SCHOLASTIC, CARTWHEEL BOOKS,

and associated logos are trademarks and/or

registered trademarks of Scholastic Inc.

ISBN-13: 978-0-439-70870-8

ISBN-10: 0-439-70870-2

10 9 8 7 6 5 4 3 2 1   08 09 10 11 12/0

Printed in Singapore

First printing, August 2008

Book Design by Walter Wick and David Saylor

FOR LINDA

Library of Congress Cataloging-in-Publication Data

Wick, Walter.

Can you see what I see? On a scary scary night: picture

puzzles to search and solve / by Walter Wick   p. cm.

ISBN 0-439-70870-2

1. Picture puzzles—Juvenile literature. 2. Haunted places.—Juvenile literature.

3. Ghosts—Juvenile literature. I. Title.

GV1507.P47W51334 2008

793.73--dc22   2007029839

CONTENTS

Can you see
what I see?
A hilltop castle,
a deer, a dragon,
a fox, a fish bone,
a horse and wagon,
3 hearts of stone,
a hatchet, a hare,
4 skulls, a cobra,
a raccoon, a bear,
a bat that slumbers,
a cat that grins—
Now brave the night;
your journey begins!

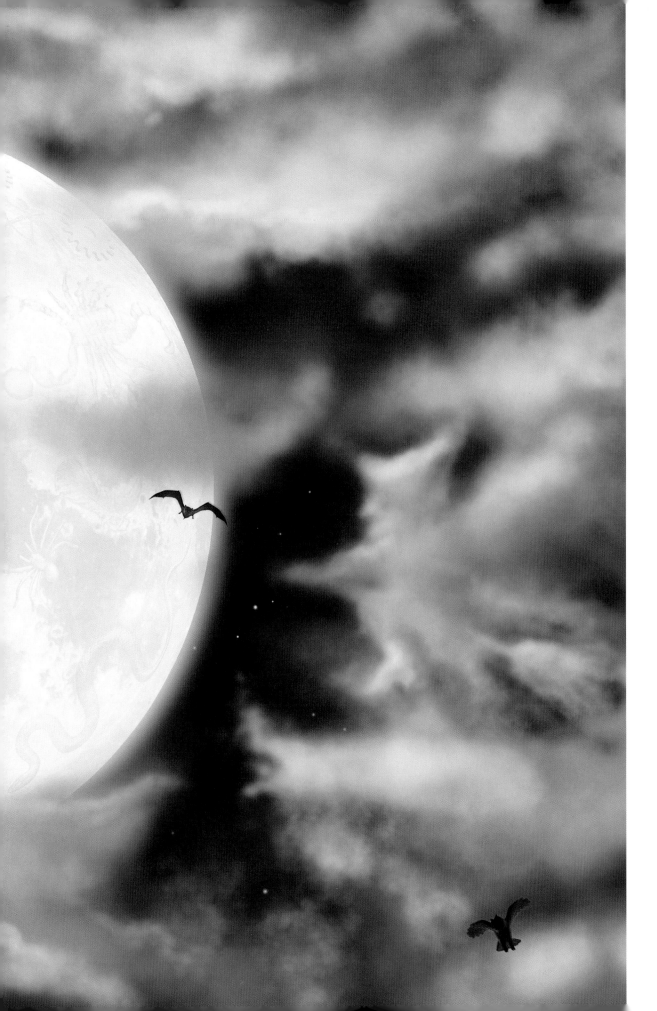

Can you see
what I see?
2 spiders, a snake,
a moth, a lizard,
a dragonfly,
a witch, a wizard,
a button, a key,
a hammer, a saw,
a frying pan
in a scorpion claw,
a beetle, 3 frogs,
a bird of prey—
And a scary moon
to light your way.

Can you see
what I see?
A bone, a bottle,
a spool of thread,
a wagon wheel,
a horse's head,
a clock, a clothespin,
a gingerbread house,
5 boats, a ladder,
a thimble, a mouse,
a howling wolf,
a scary frown—
Can you make your way
through the scary town?

Can you see
what I see?
A blue umbrella,
a duck-head cane,
a spiderweb
on a windowpane,
5 frogs, 2 bats,
a bell, a snail,
a hammer, a claw,
a long fingernail,
a frightened cat
on a windowsill—
For the next fright,
go up the hill.

Can you see
what I see?
An ax, a shovel,
a coffin, a grave,
a slippery snake,
a scary skull-cave,
a high-flying crow,
an owl, a knight,
a broom, a witch,
a black cat, a kite,
2 tree creatures,
a frog, 4 keys—
Now go to the castle
and enter, please.

Can you see
what I see?
A lizard's tongue,
2 empty frames,
3 dragonflies,
a skull in flames,
an elephant's trunk,
a clock, a key,
5 swords, a shell,
a peacock, a bee,
dinosaur footprints,
3 owls, 2 bears—
Now go past the knight
to the scary stairs!

Can you see
what I see?
A skeleton hand,
a spider, 3 rats,
a crown, 4 skulls,
a monkey, 5 bats,
a sword in a stone,
a lion, a bell,
a lizard, a lock,
a shield, a shell,
a good luck symbol,
an arrow, a crow—
Now up and up
and up you go!

Can you see
what I see?
A parrot, a crab,
2 turtles, a goat,
an ape, an acorn,
a dolphin, a boat,
3 butterflies,
a scorpion tail,
a pair of pliers,
a wishbone, a whale,
a broom, a dragon,
5 dinosaurs—
Do you dare to look
behind those doors?

Can you see
what I see?
A hungry mouse,
a skull-backed spider,
3 ships, an anchor,
a camel rider,
a skull and crossbones,
a spool of thread,
a bicycle,
a stone arrowhead,
a Cyclops skull
in a scary nook—
Now step forward
for a closer look!

Can you see
what I see?
A bony bird beak,
green glowing eyes,
a fish-head skull,
a dragon, 3 flies,
a mummy case,
a mouse, a frog,
a monkey, a moon,
a rabbit, a dog,
a windup key,
a spoon, a fork—
And a spirit potion
with a leaky cork!

Can you see
what I see?
A candlestick,
a cauldron, 5 cats,
a ghostly hand,
2 pointed hats,
a squirrel, 3 snakes,
3 monkeys, too,
a fly, a feather,
a kangaroo,
a book of magic
from another age—
For one last thrill,
turn the page!

Can you see
what I see?
A scorpion,
a screaming tree,
an hourglass,
a skeleton key,
a tiny spider,
a goose, a cat,
a princely frog,
a bee, a bat,
a wizard's wand,
a witch's shoe,
a ghost brewed in
a bottle—
BOO!

Can You See What I See? On a Scary Scary Night takes its inspiration from the classic folktale *In a Dark, Dark Wood*. In adapting the tale to a twelve-picture narrative, I sought to highlight, in visual terms, the notion of zooming in to ever-increasing details until we are beyond the range of normal vision. Beginning with a view of a distant castle on a hill and ending inside the tallest tower of that castle, the zoom ultimately focuses on a tiny bottle, whose label is magnified more than eight times its actual size ("Scary Scary Bottle," pages 30-31), revealing some three dozen details not visible in the previous spread, where the same bottle is shown actual size. Motifs borrowed from the days when sorcery mixed with science and legend mingled with fact provided an ideal backdrop for this particular adventure, where the reader encounters both the familiar and the strange and where the eye sometimes plays tricks on the mind. However, when sharp-eyed readers master this hunt, it's my hope that they discover something else, too: that just as some objects aren't what they first appear to be, most things aren't as scary as they first may seem.

Acknowledgments: I'm forever indebted to my staff members and freelance artists, without whom this book would not be possible. Studio manager Dan Helt supervised operations in the workshop, as well as provided expert technical support for computer and camera systems. Prop manager Emily Cappa kept order in the studio and provided invaluable artistic support in the workshop. A very special thanks to the freelance artists: to Randy Gilman, who sculpted the two foreground houses in "Scary Street" (pages 16-17), the spiral stair column in "Scary Stairs" (pages 22-23), the cabinet in "Scary Tower" (pages 24-25), and all the large trees for "Scary Night" and "Scary Hill" (pages 10-11 and 18-19), as well as innumerable whimsical props and details throughout the book; to Mike Galvin, who made more than one hundred miniature houses for "Scary Town" (pages 14-15), built the shelves for "Scary Cupboard" (pages 26-27) and several houses in "Scary Street," and sculpted all stone walls, cobblestone pavement, and numerous other creative details throughout the book; to Michael Lokensgaard for building the miniature room in "Scary Castle" (pages 20-21), for his help engineering the "Scary Stairs," and for his brilliant work on all the miniature landscapes. In addition, I'd like to thank Niklas Lokensgaard and Ulrich Birkmaier for lending their artistic talents. Finally, heartfelt thanks to my wife, Linda Cheverton-Wick, for her crucial behind-the-scenes support and her love.

At Scholastic, I am deeply grateful to Grace Maccarone and Ken Geist for bringing the tale *In a Dark, Dark Wood* to my attention, to Ellie Berger for her understanding and support, and to David Saylor and Stephen Hughes for their expert guidance of this book's design.

–Walter Wick

All sets were designed, photographed, and digitally composited by the author.

Walter Wick is the photographer of the I Spy series of books, with more than twenty-nine million copies in print. He is author and photographer of *A Drop of Water: A Book of Science and Wonder*, which won the Boston Globe/Horn Book Award for Nonfiction, was named a Notable Children's Book by the American Library Association, and was selected as an Orbis Pictus Honor Book and a CBC/NSTA Outstanding Science Trade Book for Children. *Walter Wick's Optical Tricks*, a book of photographic illusions, was named a Best Illustrated Children's Book by the *New York Times Book Review*, was recognized as a Notable Children's Book by the American Library Association, and received many awards, including a Platinum Award from the Oppenheim Toy Portfolio, a Young Readers Award from *Scientific American*, a *Bulletin* Blue Ribbon, and a Parents' Choice Silver Honor. *Can You See What I See?*, published in 2003, appeared on the *New York Times* Bestseller List for twenty-two weeks. His most recent books in the Can You See What I See? series are *Dream Machine*, *Seymour and the Juice Box Boat*, *Cool Collections*, *The Night Before Christmas*, and *Once Upon a Time*. Mr. Wick has invented photographic games for *GAMES* magazine and photographed covers for books and magazines, including *Newsweek*, *Discover*, and *Psychology Today*. A graduate of Paier College of Art, Mr. Wick lives in Connecticut with his wife, Linda.

More information about Walter Wick is available at www.walterwick.com.